What Were Their Names Before?

MW00979438

Real Names of More than 300 Celebrities
And the Stories They Tell

W I L L I A M   K O Z E L   &   B A R R I E   M A G U I R E

CB
CONTEMPORARY
BOOKS
CHICAGO

Library of Congress Cataloging-in-Publication Data

Kozel, William.
     What were their names before? : real names of more than 300
celebrities and the stories they tell / William Kozel & Barrie
Maguire.
        p.   cm.
    ISBN 0-8092-3773-3 (paper)
    1. Names, Personal—United States.   2. Celebrities.   3. Anonyms
and pseudonyms.   I. Maguire, Barrie.   II. Title.
CS2377.K68   1993
929.4'0973—dc20   93-2220
                                          CIP

Published by Contemporary Books, Inc.
Two Prudential Plaza, Chicago, Illinois 60601-6790
Manufactured in the United States of America
International Standard Book Number: 0-8092-3773-3
10   9   8   7   6   5   4   3   2   1

To our wives,
Karen Kludjian and Karen Maguire

Acknowledgments

The authors would like to thank Linda Gray for her creative vision in making this book possible.

We would also like to thank Karen Kludjian for her research into celebrity names and their meanings and Karen Maguire for her research into celebrity faces.

Introduction

What's in a name? Plenty. Just ask funnyman Melvin Kaminsky (Mel Brooks) or cowboy hero Leonard Sly (Roy Rogers). They're just two of the hundreds of people who have changed their names in their quest for fame.

The names we're born with, however, are an essential part of our heritage. Original names may not have marquee appeal (would we ever have followed the Yellow Brick Road behind the owner of so pedestrian a name as Frances Gumm?), but they offer a wealth of insight into their owners' ancestry, origins, appearances—even personalities and talents.

In this book, you'll learn the real names of hundreds of famous film, television, sports, political, and literary celebrities as well as the *meanings* of those names—meanings that offer a fun and fascinating look at the often surprising significance of the name *behind* the fame.

A

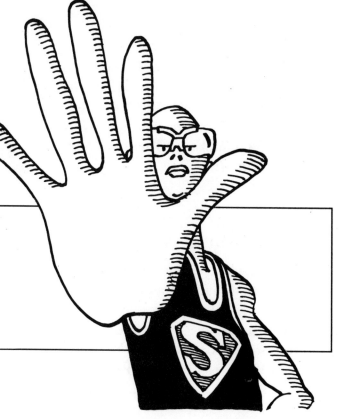

Kareem Abdul-Jabbar

Although he's best known for his brilliant offensive plays, this basketball great's real name is: **Ferdinand Lewis** *Alcindor, Jr.—"Defender of Men"*

Don Adams

As the clumsy superspy Maxwell Smart, he seldom won the praises of his Chief. But someone in his family tree must have done something right to earn the name: **Donald James *Yarmy*—*"May God Exalt Him"***

Maud Adams

When she played James Bond's love interest in the underwater thriller *Octopussy*, she must have felt right at home, because her real name is: **Maud Solveig Christina *Wikstrom*—*"One Who Lives by the Stream"***

Anouk Aimée

This star of the romantic film classic *A Man and a Woman* may seem to be the quintessential French actress, but her real name tells of a Spanish heritage: Françoise *Sorva—"From the City of Soria"*

Alan Alda

In "M*A*S*H," Hawkeye Pierce was a most unhappy resident of South Korea. But his real name speaks of a much happier life in southern Italy: **Alphonso D'Abruzzo—*"The Man from Abruzzi"***

Eddie Albert

The "Green Acres" resident who imposed his will on Hooterville comes from a long line of village leaders: **Edward Albert *Heimberger—"The Mayor"***

Sholom Aleichem

Through his writings, this "Yiddish Mark Twain" helped to perpetuate many great Jewish traditions. It's only natural for a man whose real name is: **Solomon J. *Rabinowitz—"Son of the Rabbi"***

Woody Allen

In the film world, many believe that Woody is king of the hill—an appropriate position for someone whose real name is: **Allen Stewart** *Konigsberg—"Hill of the King"*

4

June Allyson

This actress is known for her cheerful wholesomeness. So it seems natural that her real name is: **Ella *Geisman*— *"The Spirited One"***

Don Ameche

His outgoing demeanor has made him a popular actor since the days of radio. No wonder, then, that his name is: **Dominic Felix *Amici*—*"Friend"***

Ed Ames

With his big, athletic build and booming voice, it's not surprising to find that Ed's real name is: **Ed *Urick*—*"Man of Power"***

Julie Andrews

With her crystal-clear voice and squeaky-clean image, it's no wonder that this talented lady's real name is:
Julia Elizabeth *Wells*—*"Dweller Near the Spring"*

Adam Ant

Like all Punk Rockers, Adam projects a tough exterior. Underneath his cartoon-inspired stage name, you'll find more of the same: **Stewart *Goddard*—*"The Hard Man"***

Ann-Margret

This gorgeous singer, dancer, and actress is an enduring sex goddess. As it happens, her full Swedish name is:
Ann-Margaret *Olsson*—*"Relic of God"*

Guillaume Apollinaire

This avant-garde writer served as the point man for the early cubist painters, and his true name is equally sharp:
Guillaume *Kostrowitsky*—*"The Spike"*

Elizabeth Arden

For one whose name is synonymous with color and style, this cosmetics queen has a surprisingly drab name: **Florence Nightingale *Graham—"Dweller at the Gray Homestead"***

Desi Arnaz

While he and Lucy enjoyed tremendous success, the road was anything but smooth. But his full name suggests that Desi was well prepared for hard knocks: **Desiderio Alberto Arnaz y de *Acha* III—*"Dweller by the Rocks"***

Alan Arkin

Had he been taller, perhaps he wouldn't be so funny. Lucky for audiences that this comic actor was born as: **Roger *Short—"The Little Man"***

HA! HA! HA! HA! HA! HA! HA! HA! HA!

Bea Arthur

As Maude on the TV show of the same name and then Dorothy on "The Golden Girls," she has certainly thrown more than her share of zingers. In real life, her name is: **Bernice *Frankel*—*"The Javelin Thrower"***

B

Lauren Bacall

Bogey's glamorous sidekick could often turn hard and cold, which is no surprise when you learn that she was born as:
Betty Joan *Perske—"The Rock"*

Barbara Bach

Perhaps it was fate that attracted her to bejeweled husband Ringo Starr, for this gorgeous actress's real name is: **Barbara *Goldbach*—*"Stream of Gold"***

Lucille Ball

As a young starlet, Lucy's thick field of hair and curvaceous figure put her on the map. So it's appropriate that her real name was: **Dianne *Belmont*—*"The Beautiful Hill"***

Marty Balin

For many years he soared as a lead singer for the Jefferson Airplane/Starship. But his name speaks of a more sedentary nature: **Martyn Jerel *Buchwald*—*"Dweller Near the Beech Grove"***

John Barrymore

This renowned actor came from a family that is legendary for its on-screen talent and off-screen temperaments and tragedies—not exactly what you'd expect from a clan whose original name suggests a more carefree nature: **John Sidney *Blythe*—*"The Cheerful Man"***

Tony Bennett

Anyone who's heard him sing will agree that his voice is a gift from above. So it's natural that his original Italian name was: **Antonio Dominick *Benedetto*— *"The Blessed One"***

Allyce Beasley

Since pine nuts are an ingredient in pesto sauce, perhaps it was clever casting that landed Allyce the role of Miss Dipesto on "Moonlighting." Because her real name is: **Allyce *Tannenberg*— *"Dweller Near the Pine Tree"***

Jack Benny

Never one to squander resources, Benny made good use of his actual surname by making it the first part of his stage name: **Benjamin Joseph *Kubelsky*— *"Jack"***

Robby Benson

In his acting roles, Robby is always polite, even reverent. No surprise, then, that his original name was:
Robin *Segal*—*"The Priest's Assistant"*

Polly Bergen

This elegant actress rose to the heights of her profession, and stayed there for decades, so her real name fits well:
Nellie Paulina *Burgin*—*"The Mountain Dweller"*

Milton Berle

Most often, it was Uncle Milty who suffered the comic slings and arrows. But his name speaks of an ancestor who kept the upper hand: **Milton** *Berlinger—* *"The Bear Hunter"*

Irving Berlin

It's no wonder the great American songwriter lived to the ripe old age of 99. Before he came to this country, his name was: **Israel Isador *Baline—"The Healthy Man"***

Joey Bishop

He chose a stage name with religious overtones. Maybe it's because his real name was: **Joseph Abraham *Gottlieb— "Lover of God"***

Amanda Blake

As Miss Kitty on "Gunsmoke," she held her own against some pretty ornery critters. Her real name reveals a heritage of people who get their way: **Beverly Louise *Neill— "The Champion"***

Nellie Bly

When this journalist went around the world in 72 days in 1889, she was fulfilling an ancient wanderlust that is evident in her real name: **Elizabeth Cochrane *Seaman*— *"The Sailor"***

Boy George

The "Karma Chameleon" is a man of many colors. But at his core he is simply: **George Alan *O'Dowd*— *"Black"***

Victor Borge

He entertains audiences by blending beautiful music with thorny humor. A perfect profession for one whose birth name was: **Borge *Rosenbaum*—*"The Rose"***

Jeremy Brett

As the latest incarnation of Sherlock Holmes, this British actor uses his instincts, intellect, and soul to solve crimes. It seems to come naturally to one whose birth name was: **Jeremy *Huggins*—*"Man of Heart, Mind, and Spirit"***

15

Mel Brooks

He's made a career of turning icons into rubble. It must be in his blood, for he was born as: **Melvyn _Kaminsky—"The Stone Cutter"_**

Dr. Joyce Brothers

As a psychiatrist/celebrity, this charismatic lady is outstanding in her field. And, judging by her maiden name, so were her ancestors: **Joyce Diana Bauer—_"The Farmer"_**

Lenny Bruce

With his social commentary and biting wit, he left audiences in stitches. As it happens, his real name was: **Leonard Alfred _Schneider—"The Tailor"_**

Yul Brynner

In _The King and I_, he commanded respect and awe, much like the ancestor who handed down his surname: **Taidje _Kahn_, Jr.— _"The Priest"_**

George Burns

He has spent much of his career surrounded by shapely figures—not unlike his ancestors, who earned the name: **Nathan *Birnbaum*—*"Dweller Near the Pear Tree"***

Ellen Burstyn

You'd never know from her trim physique or restrained style, but someone in Ellen's past was prone to excess. Her given name is: **Edna Rae *Gillooly*— *"The Glutton"***

Richard Burton

He was a gifted actor whose voice had an otherworldly power. His given surname speaks of these talents: **Richard Walter *Jenkins*, Jr.—*"Gracious Gift of Jehova"***

C

Michael Caine

He's still as trim as when he starred in *Alfie.* But he bears the name of an ancestor of larger girth: **Maurice Joseph *Micklewhite—"The Big, Fat Man"***

Maria Callas

No one who felt the wrath of this true prima donna would believe that her real name was: **Cecilia Sophia Anna Maria *Kalogeropoulou—"The Agreeable One"***

Diana Canova

Appropriately, the star of TV's "Soap" has a heritage near the water: **Diana Canova *Rivero—"Dweller Near the River"***

Eddie Cantor

The great comedic star of the Ziegfield Follies had humor in his blood: **Edward Israel *Iskowitz—"He Who Laughs"***

Truman Capote

This great author was anything but reverent, so perhaps it's appropriate that he adopted his stepfather's name and abandoned his birth name: **Truman Streckfus *Persons—"The Parish Priest"***

Captain Beefheart

As one of Frank Zappa's bizarre contemporaries, he's often difficult for listeners to keep up with. Not so strange when you find that his real name is: **Don *Van Vliet—"The Swift One"***

Kitty Carlisle

As a singer, actress, and socialite, she is someone whose grace and style you can always depend on. So it's appropriate to find that her name is actually:
Katherine *Conn*—*"The Constant One"*

Judy Carne

On "Laugh-In," she was among the first to popularize the term *ribbit*. How fitting for one whose real name is:
Joyce *Botterill*—*"The Toad"*

Vikki Carr

She's known for her ability to shed a tear during a heartbreaking song. It must come naturally to someone whose real name is: **Florencia Bisenta de Casillas Martinez *Cardona—"Dweller Among the Thistles"***

Lewis Carroll

Beneath his imaginative writings we can see sharp social satire. And beneath his pen name, we can see where he got it: **Charles Lutwidge *Dodgson—"The Spear"***

Stockard Channing

This talented actress most likely bristles at the mispronunciation of her name as "stockyard." Indeed her real name has nothing to do with cattle: **Susan *Stockard—"Dweller Near the Fallen Tree"***

Cyd Charisse

This elegant actress practically flew across the dance floor. Her real name reveals the secret to her lightfootedness: **Tula Ellice *Finklea—"The Finch"***

Charo

She's as blond and fair as they come. Strange, when you consider that her birth name was: **Maria Rosario Pilar Martinez Molina *Baeza—"The Dark One"***

Ray Charles

He dropped his real last name, but it clearly followed close behind him in his career: **Ray Charles *Robinson—"The Famous One"***

Cher

With her daring outfits and sassy language, you'd never guess that Cher's full name is: **Cherilyn *Sarkisian—"The Saint"***

Agatha Christie

This great writer ground out mystery classics by the dozen, and her ancestry provides a clue to her prodigious output: **Agatha Mary Clarissa *Miller*—*"One Who Grinds Grain"***

Jimmy Cliff

In his defiant songs, this reggae star bows to no one. So it's not surprising that he changed his name from: **James *Chambers*—*"Worker in the Master's Quarters"***

Bill Clinton

Our forty-second president adopted his stepfather's name, which means "enclosure." But his original name is more appropriate for one who seems so open and good-natured:
William Jefferson *Blythe* IV—*"The Cheerful Man"*

Lee J. Cobb

When this dramatic actor bellowed, others looked for protection, so it's ironic that his name was actually:
Leo *Jacob*—*"May God Protect"*

Robert Conrad

When he flew with TV's "Black Sheep Squadron," he was soaring with the birds of his ancestry, because his real name is:
Conrad Robert *Falk*—*"The Falconer"*

Alice Cooper

Strip away the makeup and the wild persona, and you find that this rocker has the simplest of roots: **Vincente** *Furnier—"The Bread Baker"*

David Copperfield

Take a peek below the stage name of one who's sly and mysterious and always lands on his feet, and presto—you'll find: **David** *Kotkin—"The Cat"*

Howard Cosell

No one can equal Howard's skills as a pontificator. So it's fitting that his real name is: **Howard William** *Cohen—"The High Priest"*

Elvis Costello

When he borrowed the first name of The King of rock and roll, it was an even trade for his old last name: **Declan Patrick** *McManus—"The King"*

Lou Costello

His partner was an Abbott, but neither was particularly pious. Maybe that's why Lou changed his last name from: **Louis Francis** *Cristillo—"Follower of Christ"*

Joan Crawford

Audiences revered her. Her children feared her. So it's easy to believe that the real name behind Mommie Dearest was: **Lucille Fay** *Le Sueur—"The Respected One"*

Quentin Crisp

Anyone who can write a book called *How to Become a Virgin* certainly

deserves the name: **Denis** *Pratt—"The Cunning Man"*

Christopher Cross

His lilting music has brought a feeling of serenity to millions. Appropriately, his name is actually: **Christopher** *Geppert—"Peace"*

Tony Curtis

His dark good looks landed him starring roles in romantic comedies. It's no wonder, then, that his real name is: **Bernard** *Schwartz—"The Dark Man"*

D

Rodney Dangerfield

Perhaps the king of put-downs would get more respect if he reclaimed his original name: **Jacob *Cohen*—*"The High Priest"***

Doris Day

On the screen, she was always sweet and pure. It must have come naturally, since her real name was:
Doris *VonKappelhoff*—*"Dweller Near the Chapel"*

Jimmy Dean

Don't expect to learn the secret recipe behind his successful sausage products. It's well guarded by the man whose real name is: **Seth *Ward*—*"The Watchman"***

Yvonne De Carlo

As Lily on "The Munsters," there was nothing average about this exotic actress. But her real-life name is far more mundane: **Peggy Yvonne *Middleton*—*"From the Middle Town"***

Sandra Dee

Those who found her acting and singing to be overly saccharine will find the explanation in her real name: **Alexandra *Zuck*—*"The Sugar Seller"***

John Denver

Trade the Rockies for the Alps and singing for yodeling, and it's not hard to believe that John's original name was: **Henry John *Deutschendorf*, Jr.—*"The German"***

John Derek

Former wives Ursula Andress and Linda Evans and current wife Bo speak of a man who left no doubt as to who was boss. So does his true name:
Derek *Harris—"Ruler of the Home"*

Andy Devine

Roy Rogers's sidekick was always a paleface. But his name says otherwise:
Jeremiah *Schwartz—"The Dark Man"*

Susan Dey

From the remnants of her stint on "The Partridge Family," she managed to forge a second career as a dramatic actress on "L.A. Law," and then a third one as a comedian on "Love and War." No sweat for one whose real name is:
Susan *Smith—"The Metal Worker"*

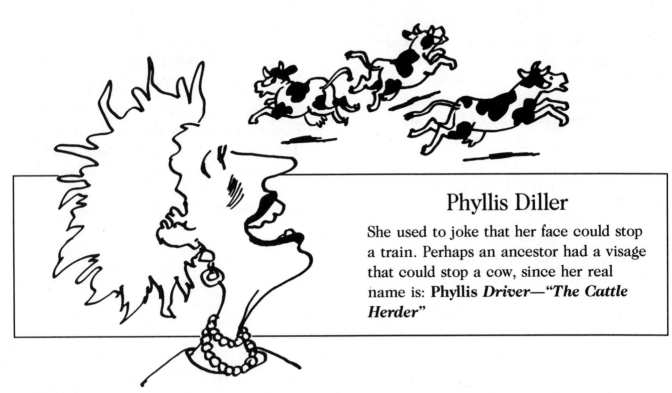

Phyllis Diller

She used to joke that her face could stop a train. Perhaps an ancestor had a visage that could stop a cow, since her real name is: **Phyllis *Driver—"The Cattle Herder"***

Dion

With a surname like his, you would think he would have been shielded from heartbreakers like "Runaround Sue": **Dion *DiMucci—"May God Protect"***

Troy Donahue

It was predestined that this handsome actor would make his parents proud, since his name was actually: **Merle Johnson, Jr.—*"The Favored Son"***

Dorothy Dix

In the early 1900s, she was the columnist to the lovelorn, but one wonders what she would have thought of today's Dr. Ruth. Especially since her real name was: **Elizabeth Meriwether *Gilmer—"Devoted to the Virgin Mary"***

Donovan

In the turbulent '60s, this gentle folk singer was a voice of calm and comfort. Appropriate for one whose full name is: **Donovan P. *Leitch—"The Healer"***

Kirk Douglas

Son Michael inherited this great actor's handsome features, right down to the cleft chin. Judging from Kirk's original name, these two are not the first to maintain a close family resemblance: **Issur Danielovich *Demsky*—*"The Twin"***

Margaret Dumont

If you're going to play straight woman to Groucho Marx, you've got to be able to take the heat. She did so with style: **Margaret *Baker*—*"Owner of the Bread Oven"***

Dr. John

With his growling voice and boogie-woogie piano, he keeps many of New Orleans's finest traditions alive. And with his long mane, he keeps a family tradition alive: **Malcolm John *Rebennack*, Jr.—*"The Man with Unkempt Hair"***

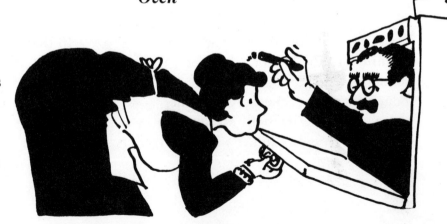

Bob Dylan

With words, notes, and his wooden guitar, he is the greatest musical craftsman of his generation. His real name speaks of a heritage of fine workmanship: **Robert Allen Zimmerman—*"The Carpenter"***

E

Sheena Easton

With her shock of jet-black hair, this singer-actress lives up to her real name: **Sheena Shirley *Orr—"The Black Rooster"***

Barbara Eden

She's best known for living in a bottle, but "Jeannie" 's real name tells of more expansive surroundings: **Barbara Huffman—*"Dweller Near the Hill"***

33

Mama Cass Elliot

In real life, this Mama had the name of a padre: **Ellen Naomi *Cohen*—*"The High Priest"***

Ron Ely

This TV Tarzan of the '60s was hard and strong—and so is his real name: **Ronald *Pierce*—*"The Rock"***

Werner Erhard

Those who believe in est say he led them to new heights, while those who don't say he led them down a primrose path. Both opinions are represented in his real name: **Jack *Rosenberg*—*"From the Rose Mountain"***

Dale Evans

Perhaps she should have made Trigger's shoes, since her maiden name is:
Frances Octavia *Smith—"The Metal Worker"*

Linda Evans

Husbands John Derek and Yanni will no doubt understand why this beautiful actress is actually named:
Linda *Evenstad—"Heaven"*

Chad Everett

This star of "Medical Center" can undoubtedly live wherever he pleases, but his ancestors clearly weren't so lucky:
Raymond Lee *Cramton—"Home Frequented by Crows"*

Fabian

From his appearances in beach-blanket movies, it's obvious that this teen heartthrob was no equal to the ancestor from whom he got the name: **Fabiano Anthony *Forte*—*"The Strong Man"***

Douglas Fairbanks

With his bride, Mary Pickford, he built one of Hollywood's most spectacular homes. A natural move for one who was born as: **Douglas *Ulman*—*"The Landowner"***

Morgan Fairchild

With her blond tresses and porcelain complexion, it's no coincidence that Morgan's real name is: **Patsy Ann *McClenny*—*"The Pale One"***

Donna Fargo

This petite country singer lives up to her birth name: **Yvonne *Vaughan*—*"The Little One"***

W. C. Fields

With his outlook on kids, dogs, and just about anything without a vintage, it's not surprising that this curmudgeon's actual name was: **William Claude Dukenfield**—*"The Gloomy Man"*

Larry Fine

Generations of Stooges fans can't be wrong! This man was born to be a legend (nyuk, nyuk): **Laurence Fineburg**—*"The Excellent One"*

Zelda Fitzgerald

F. Scott's wife was as beautiful as spun silk—and just as fragile. So it's appropriate that her maiden name was: **Zelda Sayre**—*"One Who Sold Silk"*

Ford Madox Ford

Ever wonder why this English author had the same first and last name? It was only a bluff—just like his real name: **Ford Madox *Hueffer*—*"Dweller on the Bluff"***

John Forsythe

This dashing actor's stage name means "Man of Peace." Perhaps he chose it for its closeness to his real name: **John Lincoln *Freund*—*"The Friendly Man"***

Gerald Ford

Leading the nation must have come naturally to our 38th President. Although he took his stepfather's name, his birth name was actually: **Leslie Lynch *King*, Jr.—*"One of Royal Appearance"***

Redd Foxx

Anyone who crossed Fred Sanford got an earful. But Redd's real name speaks of something that was easy to cross: **John Elroy *Sanford—"From the Sandy Ford"***

Anthony Franciosa

No one would ever confuse this handsome actor with a homely bug, but somewhere in his family tree there was someone who earned the name: **Anthony George *Papaleo—"The Beetle"***

Connie Francis

As she grew tan on the beach in *Where the Boys Are*, she was acting out a family tradition that's revealed in her real name: **Concetta *Franconero—"The Dark Complexion"***

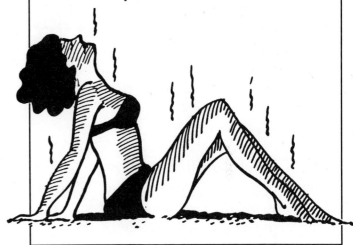

G

Kenny G

His mellow saxophone can be intoxicating, so it's appropriate to find that Kenny's full name is: **Kenny *Gorelick—"The Distiller"***

Greta Garbo

This reclusive actress adopted an Italian name meaning "The Gracious One," but her birth name belies a family tradition of keeping the world at more than an arm's length: **Greta Lovisa *Gustafsson—"Goth's Staff"***

John Garfield

As we watched him play the red-hot lover in *The Postman Always Rings Twice*, we saw the remnants of an ancient fire: **Julius *Garfinkle—"Glowing Coal"***

Judy Garland

Nothing about this complex and multitalented lady was simple—with the possible exception of her name:
Frances Ethel Milne *Gumm*—*"Man"*

James Garner

He's enjoyed a long and fruitful career, befitting someone whose real name is:
James Scott *Baumgarner*—*"The Orchard Grower"*

Crystal Gayle

With her long, silky hair, this popular singer has woven a string of hit songs. Sure enough, her real name is:
Brenda Gail *Webb*—*"The Weaver"*

Bobbie Gentry

Her "Ode to Billy Joe" spoke of a land of farms and dirt roads, but her name tells of a road more traveled:
Roberta *Streeter*—*"Dweller on the Paved Road"*

Samuel Goldwyn

MGM's tyrannical boss could certainly swim with the sharks. But underneath lurked the name of a more gentle creature: **Samuel *Goldfish*—*"The Golden Fish"***

Elliott Gould

This popular actor turned New York-style angst into a gold mine, and his name is equally rich: **Elliott _Goldstein—"Gold Stone"_**

Bill Graham

Rock's greatest impresario clearly had music in his veins, for his real name was: **Wolfgang _Grajonca—"The Violinist"_**

Betty Grable

During World War II, pinups of this leggy actress sprouted up everywhere, much like you'd expect from someone named: **Elizabeth Ruth _Grasle—"From the Grassy Meadow"_**

Cary Grant

This suave and witty actor made generations of audiences feel great, which is an appropriate role for one whose real name was: **Archibald Alexander _Leach—"The Physician"_**

Peter Graves

As Mr. Phelps on "Mission: Impossible," he was the all-American spy with a keen eye for danger. In real life, he is: **Peter *Aurness*—*"The Eagle"***

Dobie Gray

When he sings "Drift Away," he must be expressing a desire passed down from an ancestor who longed to be free: **Leonard Victor *Ainsworth*, Jr.—*"Enclosed"***

Joel Grey

Life may be a cabaret to Joel, but to a distant ancestor it was something much more sacred: **Joel *Katz*—*"The Priest"***

H

Buddy Hackett

This wacky comedian has cultivated a reputation for dirty humor, so it seems appropriate that his real name is: **Leonard *Hacker—"One Who Works with a Hoe"***

Monty Hall

The man from "Let's Make a Deal" comes from a long line of deal makers.

For proof, look behind Name Number 1: **Monty *Halparin—"The Money Changer"***

Mata Hari

This Dutch actress-spy sold her soul, and military secrets, to the Nazis, so it's fitting that her real name was: **Margaretha Geertruida *Zelle*—*"The Seller"***

Jean Harlow

The Blond Bombshell of the 1930s was precision-built for seduction, so it's appropriate that her real name was: **Harlean *Carpentier*—*"The Carpenter"***

Gary Hart

The amorous wanderings that cost Hart his political career would have been less surprising had we known his full name is: **Gary Warren *Hartpence*—*"The Stag"***

Moss Hart

When this dramatist-director braved the dreaded McCarthy hearings, it was clear that he lived up to the name behind his pen name: **Robert Arnold *Conrad*— *"The Bold Man"***

Helen Hayes

Although this actress was known for her pale skin and snow-white hair, one of her ancestors was clearly much swarthier: **Helen Hayes *Brown*—*"Dark Complexion"***

William Least Heat-Moon

His bestselling *Blue Highways* is about traveling off the beaten path, which is a

natural pursuit for one whose original name is: **William Lewis *Trogdon*— *"Dweller Near the Trough"***

Buck Henry

With his offbeat sense of humor, this writer-actor can be tart, but always palatable. Chances are, he mixes in a little of his heritage: **Buck *Zuckerman*—"The Sugar Dealer"**

O. Henry

His famous story, "Gift of the Magi," told of lovers exchanging their prized possessions. Perhaps his ancestry gave him a special understanding of material value: **William Sydney *Porter*—"One Who Carried Goods"**

Pee-Wee Herman

In his colorful playhouse, he is the perennial little kid. So it's appropriate that his real name is: **Paul *Reubens*— *"Behold the Son"***

James Herriot

This naturalist has a name befitting a defender of all creatures great and small: **James *Wight*—*"The Valiant Man"***

Barbara Hershey

Whether she plays the lover, friend, or mother in her many roles, this lovely actress is drawing on a long family tradition: **Barbara *Herzstein*—"Kind-Hearted"**

Charlton Heston

In *Ben Hur* this great actor certainly drove a mean chariot. No wonder, when you learn that his real name is: **Charlton *Carter*—*"One Who Drove a Cart"***

William Holden

In *Stalag 17*, he was the prisoner, but in real life one of his ancestors held the key to the jail: **William Franklin *Beedle*, Jr.—*"The Town Constable"***

Shere Hite

As she observes the nighttime behavior of America's couples, it must be helpful that this author's name means: **Shirley Diana *Gregory*—*"Watchful, Awake"***

Billie Holiday

Although she was known for her cool jazz vocals, Lady Day was born with a name more appropriate to one whose life became a tragic case of burnout: **Eleanor Gough *McKay*—*"Fire"***

Harry Houdini

It's ironic that the magic world's most spectacular risk taker would actually bear the name:
**Ehrich *Weiss*—
*"The Prudent Man"***

Moe, Curly, and Shemp Howard

When you make a career out of poking eyes and twisting noses, you certainly have lived up to the name of:
Moses, Jerome, and Samuel *Horowitz*—*"The Bohemian"*

Howlin' Wolf

Blues fans will agree that no one burned hotter, and perhaps it's because he was born with the name:
**Chester *Burnett*—
*"From the Place Cleared by Burning"***

49

Rock Hudson

His chiseled features were always set off by his perfectly cropped hair, so it's fitting that Rock was born: **Roy *Scherer*, Jr.—*"The Barber"***

Engelbert Humperdinck

The voice alone wouldn't make female fans swoon. It's also those swarthy good looks handed down through generations, as revealed in the name: **Arnold George *Dorsey—"The Dark Man"***

Tab Hunter

This teen idol was born to be a heartthrob, judging from his given name: **Arthur Andrew *Gelien—"The Stag"***

Betty Hutton

This star of *Annie Get Your Gun* was as beautiful as a rose, and sometimes just as prickly. Just what you'd expect from one who was born as: **Elizabeth June *Thornburg—"From the Hill of Thorns"***

I

Billy Idol

With his reputation for living on the edge, it's not surprising to find that the "Rebel Yell" boy's name is actually: **William *Board*—*"Dweller Near the Edge of the Village"***

Julio Iglesias

Should he ever tire of being a magnet for women around the world, perhaps this sexy Brazilian singer will retreat to where his ancestors began: **Julio Iglesias *de la Cueva*—*"The Cave Dweller"***

Washington Irving

His most famous tale, "Rip Van Winkle," tells the story of a man who was very much "at ease." The writer's real name tells the story of a man who was at "attention": **Diedrich *Knickerbocker*—*"The Military Man"***

J

David Janssen

As the star of TV's "The Fugitive," he was never able to stay in one town for long, but one of his real-life ancestors was clearly more settled: **David Harold Meyer—*"The Mayor"***

Robert Joffrey

His innovative troupe has served as a home to many of the century's greatest dancers. A fitting achievement for one whose name was actually: **Abdullah Jaffa Bey *Khan—"The Landlord of the Inn"***

Elton John

Today, Diet Coke may be his beverage of choice. But his name speaks of the Greek god of wine: **Reginald Kenneth *Dwight—"Dionysus"***

Don Johnson

In "Miami Vice," he tooled around in some pretty fancy chariots—especially for someone whose real name is: **Donald *Wayne*—*"The Cart Maker"***

John Paul Jones

As Led Zeppelin's bass player, he helped chart a new course for blues-based rock. His given name has equally adventurous overtones: **John *Baldwin*—*"The Bold Man"***

Tom Jones

Women fall at his feet like trees in a lumber camp, so it's not surprising to learn that his real name is: **Thomas Jones *Woodward*—*"The Forester"***

Louis Jourdan

This handsome Frenchman could charm his way into anyone's heart—and perhaps his forebears had the same gift: **Louis *Gendre*—*"The Man Who Inherited His House from His Father-in-Law"***

K

Danny Kaye

For a man of unlimited talents, he had a name that was curiously restrictive: **David Daniel *Kominski*—*"Dweller Near the Boundary Mark"***

Lainie Kazan

This exotic singer-actress seems to improve with age. She may owe it to her vineyard heritage: **Lainie *Levine*—*"The Wine Seller"***

Diane Keaton

If she seemed to be playing herself in the lead role of *Annie Hall*, it's no accident. Her real name is: **Diane *Hall*—*"Dweller in the Manor House"***

Michael Keaton

When you learn this comedic actor's real name, it's clear why he had to change it—and why he is equally adept at deeper, more dramatic roles: **Michael *Douglas*—*"The Black Stream"***

Howard Keel

When he starred in *Showboat*, this handsome actor must have felt right at home, since his stage name is actually a reversal of: **Harold Clifford *Leek*—*"Dweller by the Stream"***

Carole King

She's huge in talent as a singer-songwriter, but less imposing in physical stature—just as you might expect from one whose real name is: **Carole *Klein*—*"The Small One"***

Larry King

When you want the American people to know something, tell it to Larry King. He comes from a long line of people who make things public: **Larry Zeiger—*"Dweller Near a Signboard"***

Ted Knight

This popular TV actor was known for his booming voice and bombast, but his real name speaks in a more delicate tone: **Tadeus Wladyslaw Konopka—*"The Finch"***

Kreskin

If the Amazing Kreskin hands you a silver dollar, you can be sure he'll find a way to get it back. After all, his real name is: **George Joseph Kresge, Jr.—*"The Greedy Man"***

L

Patti LaBelle

She has a voice that can slice through a whole chorus of singers, so it's not surprising that this singer's real name is: **Patricia Louise** *Holte—"The Wood Cutter"*

Bert Lahr

The full name of the Cowardly Lion reveals his comic heritage: **Irving** *Lahrheim—"The Cheerful Man"*

Cleo Laine

Perhaps unique vocal talents run in the family, since this jazz singer's real name is: **Clementina Dinah** *Campbell—"One with a Crooked Mouth"*

Frankie Laine

Now in his eighties, this hearty singer is living up to his heritage of longevity: **Frank Paul** *LoVecchio—"The Old Man"*

Ann Landers
Abigail Van Buren

With their popular advice columns, these sisters have settled many a domestic squabble. So you might have guessed that these twin sisters were actually born: **Esther Pauline *Friedman* & Pauline Esther *Friedman*—"The Peaceful One"**

Mario Lanza

His voice continues to be a favorite in authentic Italian restaurants, which is only appropriate for one whose real name was: **Alfredo Arnold *Cocozza*— "The Restaurant Owner"**

Stan Laurel

Although Oliver Hardy may disagree, this bumbling comic genius never hurt anyone—deliberately. His gentle demeanor was true to his name: **Arthur Stanley *Jefferson*—"God's Peace"**

Ralph Lauren

"Mr. Polo" 's great sense of color has earned him a lot of green. Perhaps it's a gift handed down through the generations: **Ralph *Lifshitz*—*"Dweller Near the Lime Trees"***

Steve Lawrence

Fans of Steve and Eydie won't be surprised to find that this romantic singer's real name is: **Sidney *Liebowitz*—*"Beloved"***

John Le Carré

His spy novels are always guaranteed blockbusters—just what you'd expect from one whose name is actually: **David John Moore *Cornwell*—*"Dweller Near the Rock Pile"***

Brenda Lee

This Grammy-winning singer started her climb to fame at the tender age of six, which may have come naturally to one whose real name is: **Brenda Mae *Tarpley*—*"Dweller on the Rocky Hill"***

Gypsy Rose Lee

This queen of burlesque enjoyed a life of fame and fortune—quite unlike the humble people from whom she got her name: **Rose Louise *Hovick*—*"From the Shed"***

Lotte Lenya

A deep, sultry voice is just what you'd expect from one whose real name was: **Karoline *Blamauer—"From the Dark Swamp"***

Shari Lewis

In another life, she may have met the real Lambchop while climbing a hill, for this puppeteer's original name is: **Shari *Hurwitz—"The Mountaineer"***

Hal Linden

When taking his stage name, the star of "Barney Miller" simply traced his roots: **Harold *Lipshitz—"Dweller Near the Linden Trees"***

Little Richard

This sassy rock and roller pounded and howled his way into fame and fortune, fulfilling his ancestral heritage: **Richard Wayne *Pennimann*—*"The Wealthy Man"***

Meat Loaf

Anyone who has seen this ruddy-faced rocker perform will have no trouble believing that he is really: **Marvin Lee *Aday*—*"The Man of Red Earth"***

Jack Lord

Playing the top banana must come naturally to the star of "Hawaii Five-O,"

since his real name is: **John Joseph Patrick *Ryan*—*"The Little King"***

Sophia Loren

Her intoxicating beauty has only improved with age, so it's no surprise to discover that her original name is: **Sofia Villani *Scicolone*—*"Dweller Near the Vineyard"***

Peter Lorre

One of the great movie villains, he could be ruthless to those who crossed his path, just like his namesake: **Laszlo** *Loewenstein*— *"The Lion"*

Linda Lovelace

She became famous for activities that can't be performed while in uniform, despite the influence of her military heritage: **Linda Boreman** *Marciano*— *"One Who Marches"*

Bela Lugosi

His real name suggests that the original Dracula wasn't the first member of his family to sport oversized fangs: **Bela Lugosi** *Blasko*—*"The Man with a Speech Impediment"*

Lulu

Every ten years or so, this English singer-actress emerges with a new album. The rest of the time, she seems to revert to her roots: **Marie McDonald McLaughlin**—*"The Stranger"*

Joan Lunden

Joan's all-American looks are one reason millions of viewers find her so pleasant to say "Good Morning" to. Her real name betrays a family heritage of golden locks: **Joan** *Blunden*—*"One with Blond Hair"*

Ted Mack

On "Amateur Hour," the moment of truth was the selection of the single best performer. What a natural profession for one whose real name was: **William E.** *Maguiness*—*"One Choice"*

Shirley MacLaine

The real name of this metaphysical entertainer reveals the spiritual leanings of her ancestors: **Shirley MacLean** *Beaty*—*"She Who Blesses"*

Madonna

No one has made more liberal use of the freedom of expression, so it's no surprise that the Material Girl's full name is:

Madonna Louise *Ciccone*—
"One Who Is Free"

Marjorie Main

When she played Ma Kettle in the early television classic, this sharp-tongued actress lived up to her original name: **Mary Tomlinson *Krebs—"The Cantankerous Person"***

Malcolm X

This lanky African-American leader has grown in stature over time. So it's ironic that his birth name was actually: **Malcolm *Little—"The Short Man"***

Herbie Mann

His mellow flute playing often has spiritual overtones, so it's not surprising to find that his real name is: **Herbert Jay *Solomon—"Descendant of Solomon"***

Jayne Mansfield

This voluptuous sexpot was far from saintly. But her name implies a history of reverence: **Vera Jayne *Palmer—"The Palm-Bearing Pilgrim"***

Al Martino

He's one of the ultimate Italian-American singers, but his real name speaks with a different accent: **Alfred *Cini—"The Frenchman"***

Walter Matthau

He's a master at playing cantankerous roles, but his given name is one that suggests blessed kindness: **Walter *Matuschanskayasky*—*"Gift of Jehovah"***

Jackie Mason

Hey, if you think his humor is brutal, you should meet his ancestor: **Yacov Moshe *Maza*— *"One Who Fought with a Wooden Club"***

Robert Maxwell

This media mogul had an imposing presence that enabled him to get his way—perhaps too often. Here's the real story behind his assumed name: **Jan Ludwig *Hoch*—*"The Tall Man"***

Elaine May

When Walter Matthau left her to drown in the film *A New Leaf*, she must have felt some vibrations from generations long past, for this comedian's real name is: **Elaine *Berlin—"The River Lake"***

Felix Mendelssohn

From his name, it's clear this great composer was destined for immortality: **Jakob Ludwig Felix Mendelssohn-*Bartholdy—"The Famous One"***

Ethel Merman

When it came time for this performer to take a stage name, she simply sawed off the first syllable of her birth name: **Ethel Agnes *Zimmerman—"The Carpenter"***

David Merrick

He produced many of Broadway's greatest gems, so it's fitting that his real name should be: **David *Margulois—"Pearl"***

Joni Mitchell

In the world of folk rock, this talented singer-songwriter's appeal cuts across gender lines. Her name may explain her masculine side: **Roberta Joan *Anderson—"The Manly One"***

Marilyn Monroe

While she sometimes went by the last name of Baker, Marilyn's birth name was perhaps more fitting for a love goddess whom so many men fought for: **Norma Jean *Mortensen—"The God of Fertility and War"***

Rita Moreno

This Oscar, Tony, Grammy, and Emmy Award winner is anything but colorless, so it's ironic that her real name is: **Rosita Dolores *Alverio—"From the White Hill"***

Toni Morrison

Readers turn to this gifted author for stories of people who have braved viciousness and hardship. Her real name: **Chloe Anthony *Wofford—"Shelter from the Wolves"***

Van Morrison

The only bows this Irish singer-songwriter uses are in the occasional string section, but his ancestors had a less peaceful profession: **George *Ivan—"The Bow Maker"***

Arthur Murray

He helped millions of Americans overcome their fear of the dance floor, but his background suggests someone who was more at home on water: **Arthur Murray *Teichman—"Dweller Near the Pond"***

N

O

Juice Newton

Calling her "Angel of the Morning" may not have been so farfetched: **Judy Cohen**—*"The High Priest"*

Billy Ocean

This Caribbean singer has a name more fitting for someone whose music has a harder edge: **Leslie Sebastian *Charles*—*"From the Rock Palace"***

Odetta

Her songs speak of peace and brotherhood, but her full name speaks of more turbulent times: **Odetta Holmes Felious *Gordon*—*"Dweller in the Fort"***

Eugene Ormandy

The great conductor of the Philadelphia Orchestra had snow-white hair, just like his forebears: **Jeno *Blau—"The Pale Man"***

George Orwell

This iconoclastic author was among those who took up arms in the Spanish Civil War, so it's fitting that his real name was: **Eric Arthur *Blair—"Dweller on the Battlefield"***

P

Patti Page

Audiences flock to her because she can sing like a bird. Little do they know her real name is: **Clara Ann *Fowler*—*"The Bird Catcher"***

Joe Pass

This jazz guitar great flies up and down the frets with beauty and grace, just as you might expect from one whose real name is: **Joseph Anthony *Passalaqua*—*"The Butterfly"***

Johnny Paycheck

He became a big man in country music, but somewhere in his ancestry was a person of smaller stature: **Don *Lytle*—*"The Short Man"***

Minnie Pearl

The queen of the Grand Old Opry can trace her roots to an even more sacred place: **Sarah Ophelia Colley *Cannon—"The Clergyman"***

Bernadette Peters

For her exceptional gifts as an actress, singer, and comedian, she knows who to thank: **Bernadette *Lazzara—"Help of God"***

Roberta Peters

Conductors and audiences know they can count on this star soprano for a solid performance. Her name is one you can rely on, too: **Roberta *Peterman*— *"The Rock"***

Lou Diamond Phillips

In his movies, this young actor often plays characters who are tough, but righteous. His family heritage may explain why: **Lou *Upchurch*—*"From the Church on the Hill"***

Edith Piaf

France's beloved "little sparrow" had a heritage of living among the trees: **Edith Giovanna *Gassion*— *"Dweller Near the Oaks"***

Mary Pickford

"America's Sweetheart" was quite frail, but her real name tells of a burly ancestor: **Gladys Mary *Smith*—*"The Metal Worker"***

Iggy Pop

This early punk-rocker came from the flatlands of Michigan. But his name speaks of an ancestry on a higher plane: **James Newell *Osterberg*—*"From the Eastern Hill"***

Sylvia Porter

Her newspaper columns and books have helped millions to reap greater financial rewards. Her ancestors had a more humble row to hoe: **Sylvia *Feldman*—*"Worker in the Field"***

Stefanie Powers

Both her fans and her TV husband, Robert Wagner, would probably agree that this beautiful actress deserves the name: **Stefania Zofia *Ferderkievicz*—*"Gift of God"***

Paula Prentiss

This engaging actress was born in southern Texas, but her roots are far away, in southern Italy: **Paula *Ragusa*—*"The Sicilian"***

Robert Preston

When this Music Man measured up River City and made it his own, he was exercising a skill that ran in the family: **Robert Preston *Meservey—"The Surveyor"***

Prince

Whether you look at his first name or his last, this pop star's a real winner: **Roger *Nelson—"The Champion"***

R

Tony Randall

You'd expect this most fussy actor to be from a place where things are prim and sweet-smelling, and you'd be right: **Leonard *Rosenberg*—*"From the Rose Mountain"***

Donna Reed

This ultimate TV mom always had perfectly coiffed hair, but one of her ancestors wasn't so lucky, judging from her real name: **Donna Belle *Mullenger*—*"The Bald One"***

Jerry Reed

"When You're Hot You're Hot" may not be heavy philosophy, but this country singer must have something on the ball, judging from his fame and his name: **Jerry Reed** *Hubbard—"The Bright Mind"*

The Ritz Brothers

Compared with their ancestors, the parents of comedians Al, Harry, and Jimmy were triply blessed: **Al, Herschel, and James** *Joachim— "God Has Granted a Son"*

Della Reese

With her dual talents of singing and acting, she's reached the heights of the entertainment world. A fitting perch for one whose name is actually: **Deloreese Patricia** *Early—"The Eagle"*

Joan Rivers

Today, she's a queen of the gossip mill, but her ancestors were more inclined to separate the wheat from the chaff: **Joan Alexandra *Molinsky*—*"The Mill Owner"***

Harold Robbins

His steamy books are full of battles between lovers and others. Peel back the cover of his pen name, and you'll see the origin of his fascination with conflict: **Francis *Kane*—*"The Warrior"***

Jerome Robbins

The choreographer of *West Side Story* is also known as one of the great instructors of the art of dance. His ability to guide others may be hereditary: **Jerome *Rabinowitz*—*"The Rabbi's Son"***

Edward G. Robinson

He parlayed a plain-as-dirt mug into a rich acting career, so it's easy to see the significance of his real name: **Emmanuel *Goldberg*—*"From the Gold Mountain"***

Sugar Ray Robinson

A pounding from this champion's hot fists caused many a fighter to bend to his will. No surprise that his original name was: **Walker *Smith*—*"The Metal Worker"***

Ginger Rogers

She made a career by cutting a rug with unequaled style and grace, but it seems that her ancestors did most of their dancing outdoors: **Virginia Katherine McMath**—*"The Grass Cutter"*

Roy Rogers

America's favorite cowboy was a master of ropin', ridin', and shootin'. So it's understandable that his real name was: **Leonard *Slye*—"The Dexterous One"**

Mickey Rooney

Today, he may live among the palms of Hollywood, but his ancestors lived by more modest trees: **Joe *Yule*, Jr.— *"Dweller Near the Yew"***

Rose Marie

As Sally Rogers on "The Dick Van Dyke Show," she was known for her killer one-liners, which is in character for one whose name is: **Rose Marie *Mazzatta*— *"The Destroyer"***

Irene Ryan

Her portrayal of the cantankerous Granny on "The Beverly Hillbillies" made this actress a worldwide star. Wonder what role her ancestors played? **Irene *Noblette*—*"The Famous Person"***

Mark Russell

When he does his shtick, it's the politicians who turn red, but his own heritage is equally flushed: **Mark *Ruslander*—*"The Ruddy Man"***

Mitch Ryder

When he sings of the "Devil with a Blue Dress On," heed his warning, because this rock and roller knows what's good for you: **William S. *Levise*, Jr.—*"The Priest's Assistant"***

S

Soupy Sales

No one would ever accuse Soupy of being shy. But his name speaks of a less outspoken ancestor: **Milton *Hines*— *"The Timid Man"***

Yves St. Laurent

This enduring French designer clearly has a gift for style. Where did it come from? His real name holds the answer: **Henri Donat *Mathieu*—*"Gift of Jehovah"***

Susan Sarandon

As a portrayer of tough, sexy characters, this actress has no equal. But her name suggests otherwise: **Susan *Tomaling*— *"The Twin"***

Randolph Scott

When this hero of the westerns rode tall in the saddle, he must have felt right at home, since his real name was:
George Randolph *Crane*—"The Long-Legged Man"

Doctor Seuss

When this children's author was inventing his imaginative animals, perhaps he was drawing on the memory of the land of his ancestors:
Theodor Seuss *Geisel*—"Where the Goats Graze"

Jane Seymour

Although she was born in Hillingdon, England, this lovely actress bears the name of one born on a hill in Germany:
Joyce *Frankenberg*—"From the Hill of the Franks"

Omar Sharif

Though this handsome, charming actor has much to brag about, he refrains. From his real name, we can deduce that one of his ancestors showed less restraint: **Michael *Shalhoub—"The Boastful Man"***

Sam Shepard

His celebrity as both a playwright and an actor isn't surprising when you consider that his real name is: **Samuel Shepard *Rogers—"The Famous Man"***

Simone Signoret

With her unadorned beauty and intelligence, this German-born actress stretched the boundaries of how people defined true sensuality. It was only

86

natural for one whose name was:
Simone-Henriette-Charlotte *Kaminker—"Dweller Near the Boundary Mark"*

Beverly Sills

As anyone who has heard her sing or speak will agree, this popular performer's voice is pure sterling. And so is her real name: **Belle** *Silverman—"The Silversmith"*

Gene Simmons

Don't anyone tell this nasty, blood-spewing Kiss-man that we know the truth behind his name: **Gene** *Klein— "The Nice Man"*

Grace Slick

The lead singer of the Jefferson Airplane/Starship had a name that sounds aeronautical, but actually has a meaning even more fitting for her strong personality: **Grace** *Wing—"The Protector"*

Adam Smith

No wonder this famous 20th-century financial wizard knows the value of owning property. His name is really: **George W.** *Goodman—"Master of the Household"*

Suzanne Somers

She caused a scandal when she bared all in Playboy. Surely it's just a coincidence that her name is actually: **Suzanne Marie** *Mahoney—"The Bear"*

Elke Sommer

No doubt many a man would like to escort this sexy blond actress back to her ancestral home: **Elke** *Schletze—"From the Wet Meadow"*

Paul Stanley

Today he hammers out tunes as the guitarist for Kiss. But an ancestor was known for hammering an even heavier metal: **Paul** *Eisen—"The Iron Worker"*

Barbara Stanwyck

From her movie career to television, this
actress was always a regal presence, so
it's logical that her name was actually:
Ruby *Stevens*—*"Crown"*

Ringo Starr

His rock-solid backbeat held the Beatles
together through their most adventurous
music. It's a talent passed down along
with his name: **Richard *Starkey*—
*"The Strong Man"***

Cat Stevens

When he gave up fame and fortune to pursue a simpler life as Yosef Islam, his ancestors may have approved, since they gave him the name: **Steven Demetri** *Georgiou—"The Farmer"*

Sting

When he founded The Police, this canny singer must have known that he came from a family of law enforcers: **Gordon** *Sumner—"The Summoner"*

Sly Stone

When you discover his real name, you'll see that he was born to be the leader of The Family Stone: **Sylvester** *Stewart— "Keeper of the Household"*

Tom Stoppard

His plays are often full of interpersonal conflict, which must come naturally to one whose original name was: **Thomas** *Straussler—"The Belligerent Person"*

Donna Summer

The queen of disco knew how to seize an opportunity. It's a skill she inherited along with her name: **LaDonna Andrea** *Gaines—"The Crafty One"*

Gloria Swanson

Playing the femme fatale must have been in this actress's blood, since her birth name was: **Gloria Josephine May** *Swenson—"The Rustic Lover"*

T

Danny Thomas

Life was good to this comedian and actor, and he was good to others. So his birth name couldn't have been more perfect: **Amos Joseph Alphonsus Jacobs—*"May God Protect"***

Mr. T

He looks as big and mean as a grizzly, but underneath he's really a teddy. His real name is Mr.: **Lawrence *Tureaud*— *"The Bear"***

Arthur Treacher

He was the rock-solid foundation that kept Merv Griffin's effervescence from going over the edge, so perhaps it's no coincidence that his real name was: **Arthur *Veary*—*"Dweller Near the Dam"***

Leon Trotsky

Along with his one-time buddy Vladimir
Lenin, he was the reddest of the red. But
his real name spoke of a different color:
**Lev Davidovich *Bronstein*—
*"Brownstone"***

Sophie Tucker

She became "The Last of the Red Hot
Mamas," but a visit to her ancestral
home would have cooled her down:
**Sophia *Kalish*—*"Dweller Near the
Muddy Place"***

Tina Turner

This rock queen endured years of hardship and came back stronger than ever. Just what you'd expect from a woman whose maiden name was: **Annie Mae *Bullock*—*"The Young Bull"***

Mark Twain

In his writing and quotations Twain was often biting but never vicious. This humanistic touch is revealed in his name: **Samuel Langhorne *Clemens*—*"The Merciful One"***

Twiggy

She was among the first to announce that thin was in and hemlines were headed skyward. We heard her loud and clear: **Leslie *Hornby*—*"The Messenger"***

Conway Twitty

When he switched from rock and roll to country, perhaps he was attracted by its more reverent tone: **Harold Lloyd Jenkins—"Gracious Gift of Jehovah"**

Bonnie Tyler

This Welsh singer's hit song was "Total Eclipse of the Heart," but her name tells of one who shines right through: **Gaynor Hopkins—"Bright"**

Ritchie Valens

The singer of the hit song "La Bamba" was born in California, but his family heritage speaks of another land known for its oranges: **Richard Valensuela—"From Valencia"**

Rudolph Valentino

This great matinee idol wasn't the retiring type. So it's not surprising that he changed his name from: **Rudolpho d'Antonguolla—*"The Hermit"***

Frankie Valli

With his soaring falsetto and timeless songs, he toils in Caesar's Palace, Trump's Castle, and other modern-day houses of royalty—not unlike an early ancestor: **Francis *Castelluccio—"Worker in the Castle"***

Vangelis

His new-age compositions often sound like the music of the gods, and perhaps his Greek name explains why: **Evangelos** *Papathanassiou—"Immortal"*

Sid Vicious

This epitome of the tragic punk lifestyle had fame but squandered any hope of living up to his original name: **John Simon** *Ritchie—"The Wealthy Man"*

Gene Vincent

This popular singer was known for his wild behavior on and off stage, so it's ironic that his real name is: **Vincent Eugene** *Craddock—"The Gentle Stream"*

Bono Vox

For his stage name, the leader of U2 chose the Latin words for "Good Voice." But fans of this brainy, ethereal band will see that his birth name is equally appropriate: **Paul** *Hewson—"Man of Mind and Spirit"*

Sippie Wallace

Admirers such as Bonnie Raitt will tell you that this singer-songwriter was one of a kind—despite her real name: **Beulah *Thomas—"The Twin"***

Bruno Walter

This demanding conductor wouldn't tolerate muddy strings or soggy horns. Perhaps it's because he had come so far from his ancestral homeland: **Bruno Walter *Schlesinger—"The Swamp Dweller"***

Jack Leonard Warner

You've got to be tough to run a top Hollywood studio, and this man had some of the strongest roots you can find: **Jack *Eichelbaum—"Strong as an Oak"***

Muddy Waters

His stage name evokes the churning Mississippi delta. But his birth name speaks of a larger body of water: **McKinley** *Morganfield*— *"Dweller Near the Sea"*

John Wayne

To law abiding citizens, this all-American hero was always the man in the white hat. But the bad guys saw the other side of the Duke: **Marion Michael Morrison—*"The Dark Man"***

Raquel Welch

This sultry beauty became America's favorite bedtime fantasy. So it's fitting that her real name is: **Raquel *Tejada*— *"One with Nocturnal Habits"***

Nathanael West

This author gave us a sobering view of the American dream, so it's ironic that his true name was: **Nathan Wallenstein Weinstein—*"Wine Maker"***

Jesse White

It was only natural for this actor to play Maytag's "Lonely Repairman," because he comes from a family that lived in peace and tranquillity: **Jesse Marc Weidenfeld—*"Dweller by the Pasture"***

Wolfman Jack

He made his name by spinning vinyl, but an earlier ancestor made his by pounding hot iron: **Robert *Smith*— *"The Metal Worker"***

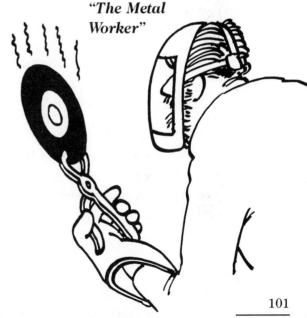

Stevie Wonder

The real name of this bold musical innovator speaks of a long tradition of derring-do: **Steveland Morris Hardaway—*"The Brave Man"***

Jane Wyman

In "Falcon Crest," she played a rich and powerful matriarch—but her real name reveals that she's just like you and me: **Sarah Jane *Fulks—"Folks"***

Natalie Wood

With her starring role in *West Side Story*, she won the hearts of millions. It was predestined for someone whose real name was: **Natasha Nicholas *Gurdin—"The Beloved One"***

Tammy Wynette

In her songs, she cries of love won and lost. So it's not surprising that her real name sings the same tune:
Wynette *Pugh*—*"Heart"*

Ed Wynn

He became famous for his meek and gentle spirit, but his name reveals an inner strength: **Isaiah Edwin *Leopold*—*"The Bold One"***